AIRWAY MANAGEMENT

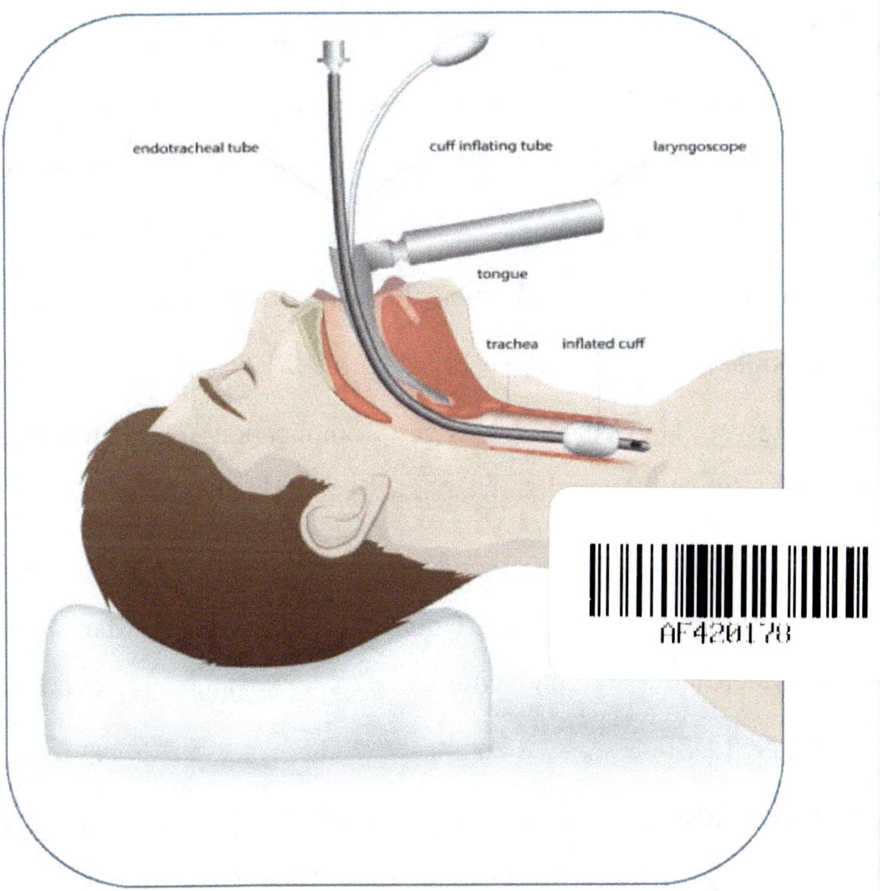

TABLE OF CONTENTS

INTRODUCTION 1

MODULE ONE 3

   LESSON: UNDERSTANDING Airway Management 3

MODULE TWO...7

   LESSON: Clinical Signs of Airway Compromise: Recognizing the Red Flags...7

Module three 13

   Lesson: Physiological Foundations of Airway Management.......13

Module four...19

   Lesson: Understanding Airway Complications Through Imaging: X-rays and Beyond..19

MODULE FIVE..25

   LESSON: Treatment Options for Airway Management: Medications and Interventions 25

CONCLUSION 32

REFERENCES..34

INTRODUCTION

The management of airways is an essential, lifesaving skill that requires not only practical expertise but also a profound understanding of the physiological and clinical signs that indicate a potential problem. Whether you are handling a simple airway issue or a complex life-threatening situation, the ability to assess, intervene, and manage the airway effectively can make the difference between life and death.

Healthcare providers are often faced with a broad spectrum of airway complications ranging from obstruction due to foreign bodies or anaphylaxis, to more chronic airway issues like asthma or COPD. Each of these conditions presents its own set of challenges, and the healthcare professional must be equipped to handle them confidently and competently. This book delves deep into the intricacies of airway management, offering insights that will help readers not only recognize the signs of airway distress but also understand the underlying physiological mechanisms that cause these symptoms. From the basics of recognizing clinical signs to advanced techniques and imaging interpretation, every lesson is packed with evidence-based knowledge that is both informative and practical.

One of the standout features of this book is its comprehensive approach to airway management. It doesn't just stop at teaching basic techniques; it goes further to cover the pharmacological interventions necessary in many airway emergencies, the role of diagnostic imaging such as X-rays in identifying airway complications, and the treatment plans tailored for chronic airway conditions. The goal is to ensure that healthcare providers of all levels can enhance their skills and apply this knowledge to their clinical practice. Respiratory therapists, in particular, will benefit from the focus on medications and treatment options specifically targeted at improving airway function and patient outcomes.

MODULE ONE

LESSON: UNDERSTANDING AIRWAY MANAGEMENT

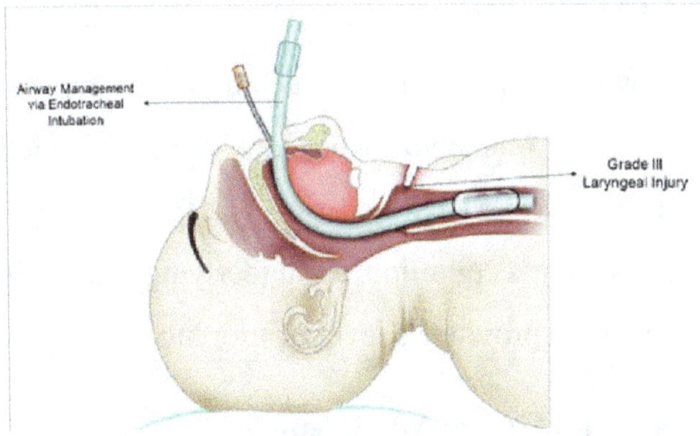

Airway management is a fundamental skill for healthcare providers across many disciplines, including emergency medicine, intensive care, and surgery. It involves ensuring that a patient's airway remains open and functional, allowing for the proper exchange of oxygen and carbon dioxide. While it might seem straightforward, the reality is that airway management can be incredibly complex, especially in emergent situations where time is of the essence. In this lesson, we will explore the basics of airway management, including why it is such a crucial skill and the various situations in which it is needed.

What is Airway Management?

At its core, airway management refers to the process of maintaining or restoring an open airway in a patient. This is critical in situations where the airway may become blocked, either partially or completely. Blockages can occur due to a variety of reasons, such as foreign body aspiration, trauma, anaphylaxis, or other medical conditions like asthma or chronic obstructive pulmonary disease (COPD). Without timely intervention, these blockages can lead to respiratory failure and, ultimately, death.

Healthcare providers use a range of techniques to manage airways, from basic manual maneuvers to more advanced methods like intubation or the use of airway adjuncts. The choice of method depends on the patient's condition, the underlying cause of the airway compromise, and the provider's level of training.

The Importance of Airway Management

The airway is often considered the most critical aspect of patient care, particularly in emergency situations. This is because, without an open airway, other life-saving measures such as administering medications or performing chest compressions become futile. A blocked airway prevents oxygen from reaching the lungs and, consequently, the bloodstream, leading to hypoxia. Hypoxia can cause irreversible damage to vital organs like the brain and heart, which is why the timely management of the airway is a top priority.

Airway management is especially important in trauma cases, where injuries to the head, neck, or chest can compromise the airway. Additionally, patients who are unconscious or under anesthesia require constant monitoring of their airway to prevent complications.

The ABCs of Airway Management

One of the most fundamental concepts in airway management is the "ABC" approach, which stands for:

- Airway
- Breathing
- Circulation

The first priority for any healthcare provider is to ensure that the airway is open and unobstructed. Once the airway is secured, the provider can assess the patient's breathing and circulation. This ABC approach is the cornerstone of emergency and critical care, providing a systematic method to ensure that all life-threatening issues are addressed in the correct order.

Basic Airway Management Techniques

For healthcare providers, the first step in managing an airway is often to use simple, non-invasive techniques. These include:

- Head tilt-chin lift: This is used to open the airway in patients who may have an obstructed airway due to the position of their tongue or other anatomical factors.
- Jaw thrust maneuver: This is often used in patients with suspected cervical spine injuries as it avoids the need to tilt the head.

- Suctioning: In cases where secretions, blood, or vomit are blocking the airway, suction devices can be used to clear the obstruction.

These basic techniques are often enough to manage airway issues in many patients, but in more severe cases, advanced methods may be required.

Advanced Airway Management

When basic techniques are insufficient, healthcare providers must rely on more advanced airway management strategies. These include:

- Oropharyngeal and nasopharyngeal airways: These are devices inserted into the mouth or nose to keep the airway open.

- Endotracheal intubation: This involves inserting a tube into the trachea to maintain a clear airway and is often performed in cases of respiratory failure or during surgery.

- Cricothyrotomy: In extreme cases where intubation is not possible, a surgical procedure known as a cricothyrotomy may be performed to create a direct airway through the throat.

MODULE TWO

LESSON: CLINICAL SIGNS OF AIRWAY COMPROMISE: RECOGNIZING THE RED FLAGS

Signs of impending airway obstruction

- Dyspnoea
- Stridor
- Stertor
- Voice change/ Hoarseness/
- Dysphagia
- Drooling/ Unable to swallow secretions
- Unable to lie flat, sitting forward to maintain airway patency

Airway compromise can happen suddenly or gradually, and recognizing the clinical signs early is vital for initiating life-saving interventions. Understanding the subtle and overt indicators of airway distress allows healthcare providers to act swiftly, minimizing complications and improving patient outcomes. In this lesson, we'll explore the various clinical signs that point to an impending or current airway crisis, as well as the underlying physiological mechanisms that cause them.

Understanding Airway Compromise

Airway compromise refers to any condition where the airway is partially or fully obstructed, making it difficult for air to pass through the respiratory tract. It can occur due to a variety of reasons, including:

- Physical obstructions: Foreign bodies, tongue positioning, swelling, or trauma can block the airway.

- Physiological factors: Conditions like anaphylaxis, asthma, and COPD can narrow the airways, limiting airflow.

- Neurological conditions: Conditions that affect the muscles involved in breathing can also compromise the airway, such as neuromuscular diseases or unconsciousness following trauma or sedation.

The key to effective airway management lies in the early identification of clinical signs, which can be divided into two categories: early signs and late signs.

Early Clinical Signs of Airway Distress

Healthcare providers should be trained to recognize the earliest signs of airway distress, as this is the most critical window for intervention.

- Increased Work of Breathing: One of the first indicators of a compromised airway is an increased effort to breathe. Patients may appear to be working harder to move air in and out of their lungs. Signs of increased work of breathing include:

- Use of accessory muscles: The patient may use neck and shoulder muscles to assist in breathing, indicating difficulty maintaining adequate ventilation.

- Retractions: Look for inward movement of the chest wall, particularly at the sternum, intercostal spaces, or under the ribcage. This can be a sign that the patient is struggling to breathe.

- Nasal flaring: In children and infants, nasal flaring can be an early sign of respiratory distress.

Changes in Respiratory Rate and Depth:

- Tachypnea (rapid breathing) is often one of the first signs of distress as the body attempts to compensate for reduced oxygen levels.
- Bradypnea (slow breathing), on the other hand, may indicate a worsening condition where the patient is tiring or has neurological impairment.
- Shallow breathing may also suggest that the airway is compromised, preventing the patient from taking full breaths.

Audible Respiratory Sounds:

- Stridor: A high-pitched, wheezing sound that occurs during inspiration, typically indicating an upper airway obstruction. It may be heard in conditions like epiglottitis, croup, or foreign body aspiration.
- Wheezing: A whistling sound during exhalation or inhalation, which is common in lower airway conditions like asthma or bronchospasm.
- Gurgling or snoring: These sounds suggest secretions or a relaxed tongue obstructing the airway, and they often require immediate suction or airway positioning.
- Patient Positioning: Patients in distress often adopt specific positions to maximize airflow.

For example:

- Tripod position: The patient sits leaning forward with arms supporting their body weight. This helps to open the airway and improve airflow in those with difficulty breathing.

- Head tilt-back or forward: An unconscious patient might tilt their head back or forward in an attempt to open the airway. This can also indicate a partial obstruction or tongue-related airway compromise.

- Restlessness and Anxiety: Patients may exhibit restlessness, anxiety, or agitation as their body senses inadequate oxygenation. These signs may be subtle, but they often indicate hypoxia. Additionally, changes in mental status such as confusion or irritability may be early indicators of hypoxemia (low blood oxygen levels).

Late Clinical Signs of Airway Compromise

Once the airway becomes severely compromised, more obvious signs emerge. These late-stage symptoms indicate that the patient is at imminent risk and requires immediate intervention.

Cyanosis:

Cyanosis is a bluish discoloration of the skin, particularly noticeable around the lips, nose, and extremities. It results from inadequate oxygenation of the blood and indicates a serious compromise in ventilation. By the time cyanosis develops, the patient is experiencing significant respiratory distress, and immediate action is required.

Altered Level of Consciousness:

Hypoxia and hypercapnia (elevated levels of carbon dioxide) can impair brain function, leading to confusion, drowsiness, or unconsciousness. If a patient becomes unresponsive or exhibits changes in their level of consciousness, airway compromise should be considered, and urgent airway intervention may be required.

Silent Chest:

In conditions like asthma or anaphylaxis, the absence of wheezing or breath sounds can be a life-threatening sign. It indicates that the patient is no longer able to move air through the airways, often due to severe obstruction or bronchospasm. This "silent chest" is a medical emergency.

Respiratory Arrest:

The most critical late sign of airway compromise is respiratory arrest, where the patient stops breathing altogether. Without immediate intervention, respiratory arrest leads to cardiac arrest and death.

Recognizing Specific Clinical Scenarios

- Foreign Body Obstruction: A sudden onset of respiratory distress, particularly in children, may indicate a foreign body obstruction. Signs to look for include:
  - ✓ Sudden coughing or choking.
  - ✓ The patient clutching at their throat.

- ✓ Difficulty speaking or breathing. Immediate intervention, such as back blows or the Heimlich maneuver, may be necessary.
- Anaphylaxis: In cases of severe allergic reactions, airway compromise can occur rapidly due to swelling of the throat and tongue. Signs include:
  - ✓ Swelling of the face, lips, and tongue (angioedema).
  - ✓ Stridor and wheezing.
  - ✓ Rash or hives. Epinephrine is the first-line treatment, followed by securing the airway if swelling progresses.
- Asthma Exacerbation: Patients with asthma may present with wheezing, shortness of breath, and chest tightness. In severe cases, they may develop a silent chest, indicating an inability to ventilate. Bronchodilators and corticosteroids are key treatments in these situations.

MODULE THREE

LESSON: PHYSIOLOGICAL FOUNDATIONS OF AIRWAY MANAGEMENT

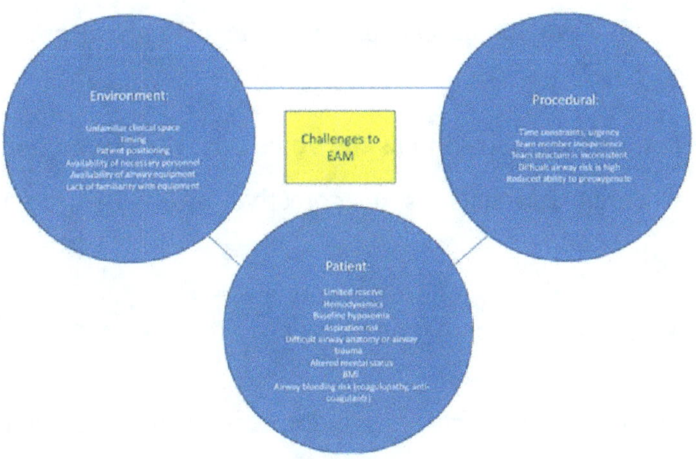

Understanding the physiological foundations of airway management is critical for healthcare providers. This knowledge not only aids in recognizing airway compromise but also informs the selection of appropriate interventions. In this lesson, we will explore the anatomy and physiology of the respiratory system, the mechanisms of breathing, gas exchange, and the impact of various pathophysiological conditions on airway management.

ANATOMY OF THE RESPIRATORY SYSTEM

The respiratory system consists of a complex network of structures responsible for gas exchange and maintaining homeostasis. The major components include:

Upper Airway:

- Nose and Nasal Cavity: These structures filter, humidify, and warm the air entering the lungs.

- Pharynx: This muscular tube connects the nasal cavity to the larynx and esophagus and plays a role in both respiration and digestion.

- Larynx: Often referred to as the voice box, the larynx houses the vocal cords and acts as a protective mechanism to prevent aspiration.

Lower Airway:

- Trachea: The trachea, or windpipe, is a rigid tube that extends from the larynx to the bronchi. It is reinforced with cartilage to keep it open.

- Bronchi and Bronchioles: The trachea bifurcates into the right and left bronchi, which lead to the lungs. These further divide into smaller bronchioles, culminating in the alveoli where gas exchange occurs.

Lungs:

The lungs are the primary organs of respiration. They are divided into lobes (three in the right lung and two in the left lung) and contain millions of alveoli, which are tiny air sacs where oxygen and carbon dioxide exchange takes place.

Diaphragm and Accessory Muscles:

The diaphragm is the primary muscle of respiration. Its contraction creates negative pressure, allowing air to flow into the lungs. Accessory muscles (such as the intercostals, sternocleidomastoid, and scalene muscles) assist during heavy breathing or respiratory distress.

MECHANICS OF BREATHING

Breathing is a complex process that involves both inspiration and expiration:

Inspiration:

During inhalation, the diaphragm contracts and moves downward, while the intercostal muscles contract, expanding the chest cavity. This creates negative pressure in the thoracic cavity, drawing air into the lungs.

The process is influenced by lung compliance (the ability of the lung to expand) and airway resistance (the resistance to airflow in the airways). Conditions that increase airway resistance (like asthma) or decrease lung compliance (like pulmonary fibrosis) can hinder effective ventilation.

Expiration:

Expiration is typically a passive process during quiet breathing, where the diaphragm and intercostal muscles relax, and elastic recoil of the lungs expels air. In forced expiration, such as during exercise or in respiratory distress, accessory muscles are used to forcefully expel air.

GAS EXCHANGE

Gas exchange occurs in the alveoli through a process called diffusion. Key concepts include:

Partial Pressure:

The partial pressure of oxygen (PaO2) and carbon dioxide (PaCO2) drives gas exchange. Oxygen moves from areas of higher concentration (in the alveoli) to lower concentration (in the bloodstream), while carbon dioxide diffuses in the opposite direction.

Oxygen Transport:

Once in the bloodstream, oxygen binds to hemoglobin in red blood cells, facilitating its transport to tissues. Oxygen saturation (SpO2) is a measure of how much hemoglobin is bound with oxygen. An SpO2 below 90% is a critical sign of potential respiratory failure.

Carbon Dioxide Elimination:

Carbon dioxide produced by cellular metabolism is transported in the blood back to the lungs, where it is expelled during expiration. Elevated levels of CO2 (hypercapnia) can lead to respiratory acidosis and subsequent respiratory distress.

PATHOPHYSIOLOGY AND ITS IMPACT ON AIRWAY MANAGEMENT

Several pathophysiological conditions can significantly impact airway management, altering normal respiratory function:

Obstructive Airway Diseases:

Conditions like asthma and chronic obstructive pulmonary disease (COPD) are characterized by increased resistance to airflow due to bronchial constriction, inflammation, or structural changes. These diseases often lead to wheezing, dyspnea, and reduced airflow, necessitating immediate interventions such as bronchodilators and corticosteroids.

Restrictive Lung Diseases:

Diseases like pulmonary fibrosis or pleural effusion reduce lung compliance, making it difficult for the lungs to expand fully. This can lead to hypoxia and necessitate supplemental oxygen and possible mechanical ventilation.

Neuromuscular Disorders:

Conditions such as amyotrophic lateral sclerosis (ALS) and myasthenia gravis affect the muscles responsible for breathing. Patients may experience weakened respiratory muscles, leading to inadequate ventilation and airway protection, requiring interventions like non-invasive ventilation or intubation.

Upper Airway Obstruction:

Causes of upper airway obstruction include anaphylaxis, foreign body aspiration, and swelling due to infections or trauma. These conditions may necessitate emergency airway management techniques, such as the Heimlich maneuver or tracheostomy.

Anaphylaxis:

Anaphylaxis is a severe, systemic allergic reaction that can lead to rapid swelling of the airway, resulting in obstruction. It requires immediate administration of epinephrine and, if necessary, airway intervention.

MODULE FOUR

LESSON: UNDERSTANDING AIRWAY COMPLICATIONS THROUGH IMAGING: X-RAYS AND BEYOND

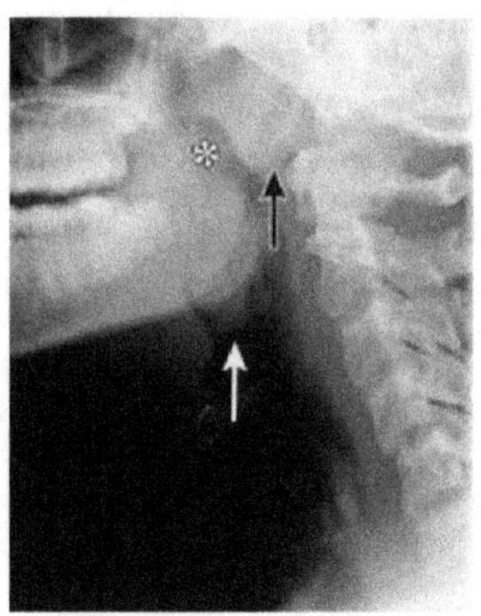

In the field of airway management, imaging plays a crucial role in identifying and diagnosing complications. X-rays, CT scans, and other imaging modalities help healthcare providers visualize the respiratory structures, assess the extent of airway obstruction, and determine the appropriate interventions. In this lesson, we will explore the different imaging techniques used in airway management, their indications, and how to interpret their findings effectively.

The Role of Imaging in Airway Management

Imaging studies are essential in evaluating patients with suspected airway complications, especially when physical examination findings are inconclusive. The main objectives of airway imaging include:

- Identifying Obstructions: Imaging helps determine the cause of airway compromise, such as foreign bodies, tumors, or swelling.

- Assessing Severity: It provides information about the extent of the obstruction and any associated complications (e.g., atelectasis or pneumonia).

- Guiding Interventions: Imaging can help guide surgical or endoscopic interventions when necessary.

X-RAY IMAGING IN AIRWAY ASSESSMENT

Plain Chest X-rays:

Chest X-rays are often the first-line imaging modality used to assess the airway and lungs. They can reveal various conditions affecting the airway, including:

- Foreign Bodies: Radiolucent objects may not be visible, but associated signs like atelectasis or air trapping may be evident.

- Airway Swelling: Conditions like epiglottitis may show swelling of the epiglottis and surrounding soft tissues, often described as the "thumb sign."

- Infections: Pneumonia and other infections may cause infiltrates or effusions, leading to potential airway compromise.

Lateral Neck X-ray:

- A lateral neck X-ray is particularly useful for assessing upper airway obstruction, especially in cases of suspected croup or epiglottitis. Key findings may include:
- Steeple Sign: Narrowing of the upper airway at the level of the larynx, indicative of croup.
- Thumb Sign: Swelling of the epiglottis, seen in epiglottitis.

Limitations of X-rays:

While X-rays provide valuable information, they have limitations. They may not adequately visualize the soft tissues of the neck or the detailed anatomy of the airways, which can be better assessed with CT imaging.

ADVANCED IMAGING TECHNIQUES

Computed Tomography (CT) Scan:

CT scans offer detailed cross-sectional images of the airway and are invaluable in diagnosing complex airway conditions. They can provide insights into:

- Tumors or Masses: CT scans can help identify neoplasms that may cause airway obstruction.
- Trauma: In cases of suspected neck or facial trauma, CT can visualize fractures and associated soft tissue injuries.
- Infections: CT scans can assess the extent of infections such as abscesses or mediastinitis that may compromise the airway.

Magnetic Resonance Imaging (MRI):

MRI is less commonly used in acute airway management but can be helpful for assessing soft tissue structures, particularly in chronic conditions or preoperative planning for complex airway surgeries.

Flexible Fiberoptic Bronchoscopy:

Although not a traditional imaging modality, flexible bronchoscopy allows direct visualization of the airway and can be diagnostic and therapeutic. It is particularly useful for:

- Removing Foreign Bodies: Bronchoscopy can be used to visualize and extract aspirated objects.
- Assessing Airway Lesions: It can help identify tumors, strictures, and other abnormalities directly.
- Interpreting Imaging Findings

Foreign Body Aspiration:

When evaluating for foreign body aspiration, look for evidence of obstruction, such as atelectasis or hyperinflation of one lung segment. Radiopaque objects (like coins) will be visible, while non-radiopaque objects may not. In cases of severe obstruction, X-rays may show mediastinal shift or displacement of structures.

Epiglottitis:

In suspected cases of epiglottitis, a lateral neck X-ray will often reveal the "thumb sign," indicating swelling of the epiglottis. The presence of adjacent soft tissue swelling may further support this diagnosis. CT scans can provide more detail regarding the extent of swelling and associated complications.

Croup:

Croup is commonly diagnosed with a lateral neck X-ray, which may show the "steeple sign." It's important to differentiate this from other conditions, such as epiglottitis, as the management differs significantly.

Tumors and Masses:

CT imaging can help characterize masses in the airway, assessing their size, location, and potential invasiveness. Radiologists look for features like irregular borders or signs of infiltration into adjacent structures.

Trauma:

In trauma cases, a CT scan can provide vital information about fractures, hematomas, or lacerations that may compromise the airway. Observing for any air leakage outside the trachea can indicate a tracheobronchial injury.

ADDITIONAL CONSIDERATIONS

Radiation Exposure:

While imaging is crucial, it's important to consider the potential risks of radiation exposure, especially in pediatric patients. Minimizing unnecessary imaging and using alternative methods when possible can help reduce exposure.

Timing of Imaging:

The timing of imaging is also critical. In emergency settings, rapid assessment of airway compromise may take precedence over more detailed imaging unless necessary for intervention planning.

Collaborative Approach:

Imaging findings should always be interpreted in conjunction with the clinical picture. A collaborative approach between radiologists, emergency physicians, and other specialists is essential for accurate diagnosis and management.

MODULE FIVE

LESSON: TREATMENT OPTIONS FOR AIRWAY MANAGEMENT: MEDICATIONS AND INTERVENTIONS

Advances in airway management in recent 10 years	
Definition	physiologically and subglottic difficulty airway
Guideline	2022 ASA and 2019 DAS
Evaluation	anatomical and ultrasound assessment
Ventilation	SJOV, HFNO and ECMO
Device	visual endotracheal tube, laryngoscope, SAD, stylets and flexible scope
Monitoring	tube cuff pressure, tube position and diaphragmatic function
Training	eFONA and gastric ultrasound
AI	assistance with intubation

Effective airway management often requires a multifaceted approach that includes medications, procedural interventions, and supportive measures. This lesson will explore various treatment options available to healthcare providers for managing airway compromise, highlighting indications, contraindications, and potential complications.

MEDICATIONS FOR AIRWAY MANAGEMENT

Bronchodilators:

Bronchodilators are critical in the management of obstructive airway diseases such as asthma and COPD. These medications work by relaxing bronchial smooth muscle, leading to airway dilation and improved airflow.

- Short-acting beta-agonists (SABAs): Drugs like albuterol provide rapid relief of bronchospasm and are commonly used as rescue inhalers.

- Long-acting beta-agonists (LABAs): Medications like salmeterol are used for long-term control and prevention of bronchospasm, often in conjunction with inhaled corticosteroids.

- Anticholinergic agents: Ipratropium bromide is an anticholinergic medication that helps dilate airways and is often used in combination with beta-agonists.

Corticosteroids:

Corticosteroids are anti-inflammatory agents that play a crucial role in managing airway inflammation, particularly in asthma exacerbations and anaphylaxis.

- Systemic corticosteroids: Oral or intravenous administration of corticosteroids like prednisone can reduce airway swelling and improve respiratory function over days.

- Inhaled corticosteroids: These medications, such as fluticasone and budesonide, are used for long-term control in chronic airway diseases.

Antihistamines:

In cases of allergic reactions or anaphylaxis, antihistamines can help mitigate symptoms by blocking the effects of histamine.

- First-generation antihistamines: Diphenhydramine may be used in acute allergic reactions but can cause sedation.
- Second-generation antihistamines: Medications like loratadine or cetirizine have a lower sedation profile and are useful for chronic allergic conditions.

Epinephrine:

Epinephrine is the first-line treatment for anaphylaxis. It works by stimulating alpha and beta-adrenergic receptors, leading to vasoconstriction, bronchodilation, and decreased vascular permeability.

In severe cases, repeated doses may be necessary, and intravenous epinephrine may be required in life-threatening situations.

Sedatives and Analgesics:

In some cases, sedation may be necessary for airway procedures or to manage anxiety. However, care must be taken as sedatives can compromise airway reflexes and breathing.

Medications like midazolam or propofol can be used for sedation, while ensuring adequate monitoring of airway status and respiratory function.

PROCEDURAL INTERVENTIONS

Airway Maneuvers:

Simple maneuvers can be performed to clear the airway or improve ventilation:

- Head-Tilt, Chin-Lift: This maneuver helps open the airway in unconscious patients by repositioning the tongue.
- Jaw-Thrust Maneuver: This is used in suspected spinal injury cases, as it does not require neck extension and can help secure the airway.
- Suctioning: In cases of excessive secretions, suctioning may be necessary to maintain airway patency.

Non-Invasive Ventilation (NIV):

Non-invasive ventilation techniques, such as CPAP (Continuous Positive Airway Pressure) and BiPAP (Bilevel Positive Airway Pressure), can assist patients with respiratory failure without the need for intubation.

These methods improve oxygenation and reduce the work of breathing, especially in patients with COPD exacerbations or cardiogenic pulmonary edema.

Endotracheal Intubation:

In cases of severe airway compromise, endotracheal intubation may be necessary. This procedure involves placing a tube into the trachea to secure the airway and provide mechanical ventilation.

- Indications: Intubation is indicated for unresponsive patients, those unable to protect their airway, or patients with severe respiratory distress.
- Complications: Potential complications include injury to the vocal cords, esophageal intubation, and ventilator-associated pneumonia.

Tracheostomy:

A tracheostomy is a surgical procedure that involves creating an opening in the trachea to facilitate ventilation. It is typically reserved for patients requiring long-term airway support or in cases where intubation is not feasible.

- Indications: Indications for tracheostomy include prolonged mechanical ventilation, upper airway obstruction, or significant facial or neck trauma.
- Complications: Possible complications include tube displacement, infection, and injury to surrounding structures.

Bronchoscopy:

Flexible bronchoscopy allows for direct visualization of the airway and can be used to remove foreign bodies, assess airway lesions, or facilitate suctioning.

It can also provide therapeutic interventions, such as balloon dilation for strictures or stent placement for airway support.

SUPPORTIVE MEASURES

Supplemental Oxygen:

Providing supplemental oxygen is a fundamental aspect of airway management, especially in hypoxemic patients. Supplemental oxygen can improve SpO2 levels and alleviate symptoms of hypoxia.

Positioning:

Proper positioning of the patient can optimize airflow. Elevating the head of the bed or placing the patient in a semi-upright position can improve respiratory mechanics and enhance oxygenation.

Monitoring:

Continuous monitoring of vital signs, including respiratory rate, heart rate, and SpO2 levels, is critical in patients with airway compromise. Early detection of changes can facilitate timely intervention.

Education and Support:

Patient and family education on recognizing the signs of airway compromise and when to seek help is essential for effective management. Providing emotional support and reassurance can also alleviate anxiety in patients experiencing respiratory distress.

The management of airway compromise requires a comprehensive understanding of available treatment options, including medications, procedural interventions, and supportive measures. By tailoring the approach to the individual patient's needs, healthcare providers can optimize airway management and improve outcomes.

CONCLUSION

Airway management is a fundamental skill for healthcare providers, encompassing a wide range of knowledge, techniques, and interventions essential for patient survival in both routine and emergency settings. This book has covered the critical aspects of airway management, from understanding the anatomy and physiology of the respiratory system to identifying clinical signs of compromise and interpreting diagnostic imaging. The comprehensive discussion of medications, interventions, and supportive measures equips respiratory therapists, doctors, and nurses with the tools to handle airway challenges confidently and effectively.

Successful airway management requires not only technical skills but also critical thinking, adaptability, and the ability to anticipate complications. By integrating clinical assessments with evidence-based interventions, healthcare providers can significantly improve patient outcomes. Whether dealing with routine respiratory care or acute airway emergencies, a strong foundation in airway management ensures that patients receive the best possible care.

As the field of medicine evolves, so too will the strategies for airway management. This book has aimed to provide a thorough and practical understanding of current best practices, while also encouraging readers to stay informed about new advancements in technology and treatment modalities. By continuing to learn and refine these skills, healthcare providers will remain at the forefront of airway management, ensuring that they can deliver life-saving care when it is needed most.

REFERENCES

American Heart Association. (2020). 2020 *American Heart Association Guidelines for Cardiopulmonary Resuscitation and Emergency Cardiovascular Care*. Circulation, 142(16_suppl_2), S337-S357.

Bledsoe, B. E., Porter, R. S., & Cherry, R. A. (2018). *Paramedic Care: Principles and Practice* (Vol. 5). Pearson Education.

Broaddus, V. C., Mason, R. J., Ernst, J. D., King, T. E., Lazarus, S. C., Murray, J. F., & Nadel, J. A. (2016). Murray & Nadel's *Textbook of Respiratory Medicine* (6th ed.). Elsevier Health Sciences.

Doyle, D. J., & Goyal, M. (2021). *Airway Management in the Critically Ill. Oxford University Press.*

Gawande, A. (2012). *The Checklist Manifesto: How to Get Things Right. Metropolitan Books.*

Hardman, J. G., & Brown, A. M. (2016). *Airway Management: Principles and Practice. Cambridge University Press.*

Kacmarek, R. M., Stoller, J. K., & Heuer, A. J. (2016). *Egan's Fundamentals of Respiratory Care (11th ed.). Elsevier Health Sciences.*

Kline, J. A. (2017). *Clinical Methods in Respiratory Care* (3rd ed.). Mosby Elsevier.

Miller, R. D., & Cohen, N. H. (2020). Miller's Anesthesia (9th ed.). *Elsevier Health Sciences*.

Walls, R. M., Murphy, M. F., & Luten, R. C. (2018). *Manual of Emergency Airway Management* (5th ed.). Lippincott Williams & Wilkins.

www.ingramcontent.com/pod-product-compliance
Lightning Source LLC
Chambersburg PA
CBHW060925130726
48001CB00006B/2418